BREAD OF

BREAD OF

Gabrielle Joy Lessans

++

ORNITHOPTER PRESS PRINCETON

"There is but one global healing [...]

Only the discovery of our interior God can heal us forever. The rest consists,

for better or worse, of beating around the bush."

—Alejandro Jodorowsky

First Edition

Published by Ornithopter Press
www.ornithopterpress.com

ISBN 978-1-942723-10-3

Library of Congress Control Number: 2021937893

Design and composition by Mark Harris

CONTENTS

BREAD OF

[SHE WOULD AWAKE AT FIVE IN THE MORNING]

++

You close your eyes: a glowing rectangle. You keep your eyes closed: it is still there, fainter, but more defined. You do not know what this means but you have a feeling. You do not like feelings like these. You demand to know in clear words, immediately. Nothing comes so you say *okay then, I'll wait to be sure. I'll wait to refine. I'll wait.*

[A GHOST OUT OF THE PAST]

++

The ground splits open. You are in suspension on your mattress. Inside of the crevasse, you look at you within the pinching axis of the hourglass. A warm germ of fluid snags up your spine. You cannot get right in your body. A flash of abstraction lands in your skeleton: *you spend too much time in your bed.* You jump to the floor. The tile is cold on the skin of your knees. You cave your palms into tiny tents & press your fingers into hard ground. Arc & bow the neck. You take our first breath.

[SHE LOOKED LIKE A NEWBORN OLD WOMAN]

++

Through the long night you went on. Being moved like the rest of your species by the opaque invisible hand. Bending blindly into new shapes which are more so somehow old shapes. You trace patterns of lineage down sidewalks with your feet. Your summer professor squints his eyes at you. You squint your eyes too, but the spirit tells you to laugh. You laugh, but never unknot your shoulders. You laugh, but only to your Self.

[HER ONLY DREAM WAS TO DIE OF FATIGUE]

++

[ONE AFTERNOON WITH A THREAT OF STORM]

++

You are mostly by yourself. You find this Self suddenly ravenous, rummaging through the kitchenette of a New York City dorm room, searching for a trace of nutrients. The fridge is empty but for your roommate's leftover burrito. The pills are wearing off. Or else your hunger is howling through all these layers to be tended to. You want to tend it, too. In the cabinet is a bag of nuts & seeds you bought yesterday from a corner store; one of those with rows of plastic bins full of trail mixed bird food. You love The City for this & mostly only that: the ability to be a little bird. To sit on benches & make harmony with whoever is lounging on the grass. Exchanging sound instead of name. You deflect marriage proposals. Accept the cold edamame. We are sacred strolling the streets alone. You don't need to feel scared because of what's becoming inside the chest. Sometimes you get scared of what is becoming inside the chest, but it feels unnegotiable: one day you'll *get up & fly away.*

[SHE FOLLOWED THE THREAD OF BLOOD]

++

You are on top of a mountain. You close your eyes & the wind stops. You open your eyes & the force of your lashes lays a gust that spins outwards, through umbral wheatgrass, a gentle riptide. You do not know the name of this mountain, but it feels tired & familiar as though these are exactly your laterals; as though this here is precisely your galactic longitude. As though even when you inevitably fall, the pinnacle of your essence will remain here at the peak, while the rest of you unravels into slighter & slighter filaments of self. Spinning out into your far fibrils. Spin until. You only resemble someone.

[SHE LACKED COURAGE TO DROWN HER IN THE BATHROOM CISTERN]

++

You like the way you look in your own mirror. So much you cower to enter the world with all her phones & cameras & storefront glass windows & now disappointing reflections of you. You marvel at the concept of the real you. At being pulled & stretched out & stunted involuntarily stimulated, back bent & condensed along an arbitrary spectrum of refractory surfaces. Still, you'd prefer the opposite; for the assurance to come from the outside; at a later point in the night; from a glimpse of the bar's back ledge or like a wink in the taxicab rearview as you're taking yourself home.

[SHE REPENTED OF HER WEAKNESS]

++

You wait until your roommate leaves to spend the night at her boyfriend's place. At this point, she leaves almost every night. You are jealous but not unhappy for her. Just jealous, as a general state of being. As in *within* jealousy. As in, it becomes your favorite window to look through but you're certain there are other windows too. And though you don't these days choose often to look through them, they are important in their persistent existence. And anyway, you so enjoy being alone, especially at night, when there is time to do the things you only can do when no one else is in the other little alcove of your small dorm room, on the top floor of the old Gothic building. Your fingers tingle every single time you move to start; as though the guilt is a compulsory aspect of the act; an inevitable additive to a stimulant that would never otherwise be pure anyway. You do not feel pure when you participate in this ritual; you do not feel comforted by the notion of others doing the same, alone, in their own dorm rooms, in stale pools of their own brands of egoic sorrow or pride. But the website already is undeniably viral; it's open forum for anonymous gossip running rampant through the minds & mouths of everybody on campus. Bodies torn from faces names listed tits rated asses praised friends slandered freshman ranked scrutinized analyzed terrorized idealized picked apart pieces put to broadcasted domain. To not keep up with the vortex is impossible. And therefore logging on is normal, something everybody does but doesn't talk about, like masturbation but without the happy ending. At least for you. At least you know how to make yourself come. At least always for as long as you can remember you have known how to make yourself feel alive. But now you can't resist this new temptation. To the chorus of a grating self-mutilation, you type the URL into the browser, soften your eyes, prepare for the imminent blow.

[BUT SHE COULD NOT PREVENT THE EXECUTION]

++

Your ex-boyfriend's older cousin—alleged queen of campus, and the only person in the whole state you vaguely knew before coming here—had told him you'd have no problem fitting in. As in, no problem *getting* in. She said that you'd be in & he told you she'd look out. You call your ex on the phone & sob: *you said she said that.* You said so, transferring all betrayal unto him. I'm sorry, he says softly & his being feels so far from you suddenly. You hang up & wonder what you did. What you didn't do. If someone did it to you & who. Your friend suggests that maybe you were blackballed, like your cool friend who fought someone's older sister on a party bus. *Can you think of anything you said; anyone you accidentally last semester did?* This feels unlikely. You are fully aware of all the people you almost did and mostly didn't do. Never black out like your friends do. Never act out unless trying to. How embarrassing a clue. You sink into the alcove of the old building where your extra-long bed is shoved. The ceiling arches above your body in protective cradle. You pull your knees up to your chin & closer whenever the phone vibrates. You are in a deep haze of sorrow that feels so indulgent it is almost akin to calm. Almost nostalgic, like the state you used to seek actively, when in the third grade you obsessed over genocide. Tore through books, devoured films just to reach. Just to ache. That sacred state of despair. No one should ever disturb such a state. You do not disturb you. Rock yourself into numb cocoon.

[A DEEP DEPRESSION FORMED BETWEEN HER BREASTS]

++

Your friends console you again and again. Your roommate promises to figure out the culprit. You make a big show of shrugging. *They fucked up big,* they all agree, and walk off to chapter together. You walk the other way down the corridor, wrap yourself in invisible shrouds of way too cool to care. *This antiquated system is for losers,* you tweet from a secret account to strangers. You wish you weren't a loser; you wish you weren't a stranger; you wish you were cool enough not to care.

[SHE FELT HER BONES FILLING UP WITH FOAM]

++

I have good news, your roommate says: *it was nothing personal.*

You just slipped through the cracks.

[SHE HAD TO GUESS DISTANCES IN THE DARKNESS]

++

Sh.

Sh.

[SHE COULD ONLY BE RESCUED]

++

At the bar, you & new friends take a shot ***to truth*** & they tell you how ***truly you dodged a fat bullet.*** You have this vague feeling the bullet was instead lodged somewhere in
your low back where upon unexpected impact it shattered
into a million tiny shards which are now
scattered for eternity
within & around
your tissue,
but you
don't share this.
You nod & repeat:
I dodged a fat bullet
& you all
raise another
into the air.

[IN THE HAZE OF CONVALESCENCE]

++

Re ach e.

[OF WHOM THERE HAD NEVER BEEN ANY NEWS]

++

When an object is observed it becomes denser; as though in affirmation; reality is sure of you. Under the gaze of an eye, matter rakes itself knowingly into more mass. Compacts. Time unfolds into linearity. Is this really what you seek? *How could I know*—you shrug toward me—*what I want.* You are turning away from me with every passing word. You do not have to know & you do not have to want, but darling do not turn. Away from me you crawl, into your bed in the hole-in-the-wall & get under a blanket & pull your knees up over a pillow & open the web browser & scroll. You scour through names upon names. You are less dense than whatever's in the back of your own closet, crumpled up, forgotten about. To be forsaken you would've once had to be held. You are the cat that does not like to be seen but needs to feel seen. That in spite of itself walks before you. You do not see it. You do not see your name anywhere on this list. You can barely remember how to spell it. Unsure if you would recognize your own letters. The cat presses lightly its black paws into the tops of your thighs. You do not notice. You do not grieve because it's more of a slipping sensation. You do not reach out to gently pull its tail.

[SINCE THAT DAY WHEN SHE BECAME AWARE OF HER OWN NAKEDNESS]

++

S h.

A c h e.

[SHE BURIED HER BODY IN A SECRET PLACE]

++

You are stuck in the same burnt feeling so much that it permeates; orange from your pores; that it fumes & seeps from the bottom of the door; that it lingers. Hovering about you as you move around campus. From your bed to the dining hall, to the classroom back to bed. You swallowed, impermanent cloud, you. Yearn to know your name. You search through every strand that might contain it. Perhaps someone accidentally saw you, your body out of or in relation to, disappearing behind, between. Perhaps that someone didn't look away.

[SHE DECIDED TO RESOLVE THE SITUATION IN A PLEASANT WAY]

++

You cross into opaque light and that thick dank smell you know too well. You are only halfway in the hallway but already it sticks to your hair, your clothes, searching your pores for more vestigial purity to raid. The insides of your nostrils sour. You check your coats at the coat-check & throw dollar bills into the pitcher because money is a construct here. Your friend is already around the corner inside the enormous wingspan of an athlete, whose infamy you know by his gravitas. You quick scan the stumbling organism of bodies all beading with booze and sweat. *He* is not here though he texted you he'd be here, but you are used to his frequent schisms. You are unperturbed by these half-truths; after all, you are nonchalantly feminine so effortlessly chill so unbothered by the dichotomy of endless streams of lustful texts & the way he publicly ignores your whole existence. Despite yourself, you do wish he would just walk up & embrace you. But you tell yourself you want nothing of such a scene. Instead you corroborate the secretion; you harbor the glimmer in private; quietly nurture the vile sieving. You peel off into the bathroom, sigh into the back of a five-person line. Try to avoid your own eyes in the half-fogged mirror; they are bored & smudged with coal. You wait & tap lightly your boot upon the floor. You sink into yourself another layer. Let hair obscure vision. You do not wish anything because this is simply where you are. One day you might be elsewhere, it could be nothing just the same.

[IGNORING THE ALGAE OF HER ANXIETY]

++

In here you refuse to let anyone access you. In here you have learned to grow tall walls of dark wood which match the pillars of the bar; which do not stand out as obvious; which you've dangled in tangles of ivy for flare. The blare of the sound system makes your ivy rattle rattle. This becomes your social sound. You rattle rattle through modules of people, steal a glance across the room and run into a body quite literally. A slop of Jameson spills onto your pants. You are embraced before you can look up. It is a vague friend who is everyone's acquaintance. The one who has more than once woken you up, uninvited in your bed; drunken fingertips exploring the seams of your underwear. *Don't worry,* you and your friends all tell each other whenever this happens to anyone on your floor, *he does that to everyone.* It honestly does not worry you, though you begin to lock the doors at night. Anyway, he's a solid face to run into at the bar. Easy to shoot the shit with. He shoots the shit & you rattle rattle hearing only about one third of the shit he's shooting; you smile through. *Yeah,* you laugh & smile the shit away. When the moment comes perfect you fade into bodily abyss.

[BUT THE DARK CLOUD BARELY PERMITTED HER]

++

He is here, you realize he is just right over there. You edge up to the bar & wait passive for a drink while bartender hands throngs of athletes free shots. You are next to get served; but not by her. Antsy; but in no rush. You try not to let your thoughts scatter instead your eyes wander towards the opposite corner. Accidentally he is staring straight at you. Warm lock. Raw surge. Such jagged recognition; you make to mouth your secret *hi* but inside the impossible space of one unuttered syllable he has already turned his dark fixation towards the low vee standing next to him. The girl behind you orders a vodka soda over your shoulder. Out of instinct you pull out your phone; try to find him there; try not to stare at the blank screen; try not to wonder if you are the one who is not here or why blue everything is so lazily turning as blankly you shift your self behind the wooden pillar; you dis appear your face into the gnaw ing of the hour.

[NOR HER CROWN OF ORANGE BLOSSOMS]

++

Morning; he appears on your screen like

last night

just some bad dream; *baby,*

I miss you; & you miss you too.

Curtailed schisms of the insides.

Cacophonic organs.

Hurriedly; hungrily; dripping; you're swallowed.

[EXILED FOREVER FROM THE DIAMOND LIGHT]

++

Sh. Sh

Sh

of the

Sh Sh

of

the Sh

[SHE GAVE NO EXPLANATION]

++

The professor smiles. You smile a smile that knows a coming doom. She does not teach in a tongue your brain can well understand. You're usually able to understand. You're always approximately competent; often more than so; rectangularly *good* at most things you do. But now you are encrusted in an artificial landscape; a numerically languaged universe composed through rigid logic & precise degree. You are not a linear thinker, and as it stands, you are left with no fissures to slide through. You go into a panic. You must pass you panic you freak the fuck out you must pass must pass this class to graduate you panic you must you must graduate you must allow yourself finally to leave.

[SHE HAD A PREMONITION THE POT OF SOUP WOULD BOIL OVER]

++

Once you read about the old bum by the railroad track—the one who eats tuna out of half opened cans & drinks the equivalent of gasoline & stands on his head for minutes a day & because of this has no jaundice or disease & is a certified eye-witnessed modern day buddha—you are electrified by the idea of yoga. So you can one day stand on your head everyday. You drop into a beginner class at the nearest studio, try to follow cues towards focus but end up thinking only about last night; how he schismed into scary; your tits now tender purpled pears. You spend the session obsessing over whether the intuitive teacher can tell. You decide instead of class to order sutras off the internet. You can read & think & understand much better than you can feel these days you've tried to render yourself incapable of most sensation, inept to any promise of real pleasure, a hopeless symbol of yourself & the endlessly enduring pain you only occasionally admit to. If you are not able to feel, you wonder why is there still so much pain. If you are not wanting to feel you wonder why you are trying yoga anyway. Besides, folding your body in half is hardly an option when your middle refutes you, and besides, running burns more calories, helps to keep your joints numb, and besides, you have way too much to do to spend an hour & a half inside your body. No; you will read the heart sutras & the kama sutras & the diamond sutras & intellectualize your way into the yoga instead. You will read the vedas & the bhagavahad gita you got this summer at that festival, from the dude with greased hair who looked into your eyes and said *I see you already know &* you smiled mellow back until your friends pulled you away & you were glad because the man troubled you because he had those matching dinner plate pupils & a trebled kind of resonance you could so readily fall into.

[SOON SHE HAD BEEN TAKEN PRISONER]

++

What do you do when you're alone, my darling? Feet embarrassed by the immediacy of the pull. You have not been dreaming about this for weeks on end, you pretend. But this is no time for deceit. You know as well as I do: this is your one maniacal chance. Molecules of glass decide to fit together better; a *clack* comes from the window; the atmosphere nears a still. There is no such thing as reprieve. I whisper a psalm into your ear but you are yet too fragile, too delicate to take on the awe of me. Ligaments unable still to leap to where the mind has dared at times already to soak. Your body will have to play linear, until nerves learn to handle this lightening. There is no chance of retreat. You turn deliberately to the right, away from my voice, into the bathroom, open the medicine cabinet, wrap your fingers around the massive container of pills. Hold your breath, listen for the door.

[IN THE BEWILDERMENT OF HER YEARS]

++

The mattress has sunken in an imprint of your body; it is known to your friends as *the womb.* You try to fall asleep in new shapes; shifting direction, position, mutation. But you always end up inside the same soft hole; the weight of you deepening the furrow.

[SHE DREAMT A DREAM THAT WAS NOT A DREAM]

++

Something is coming for you.
Hovering over. You cannot access your own
cement lidded chest; blighted heave; fail to push; heave
heave; heav y gas o lean middle
of the dry un dream ed
lungs felt of wa ter
sound less scream; sieve; hush
huh; sh; s i eve.

[SHE MANAGED TO STERILIZE HER OWN MEMORIES]

++

You almost tragic vessel of a thing.
You find your lace panties on the floor. You cannot find
heel, breath, tampon string.
You can not find a number on the door.
The terrace is silent as
you slip out. You will wait,
you decide, for a context.
You will wait, you decide,
to break down. You will not break
down because you can not
be sure. Of what or of whom
& if so, how & even so, why
cry, why start now.
You almost tragic
vessel of a thing, you.

[SITTING IN THE WICKER ROCKING CHAIR]

++

Ache.

Ache.

[LET THE OUTPOURING OF MISERY FOLLOW ITS COURSE]

++

The next day you decide not to sober. No one brushes your hair. You push push push it under the rug & join the club. Today, there is a party. Today, there is a felt costume of a crustacean and for no reason, you are now wearing it; shelled; shallowed; swallowing whatever you're handed, hanging your top half out of the sunroof of the car in some smeared pre-memory of the present. The car pulls in & the crowd cheers. You wave your red felt claw. *Hello, hello,* what is left of you is here and here is a field full of faces, names. Here is fun, can you hear it being had? You tell yourself to drink and you drink and drink and leap and run into a high school face that says: *you look great.* You know what *great* means; red; hollow; hardened like a shed husk. Starving for a gone self. Within a few hours, you are squinting at the small screen of a friend's phone. He is all glee & mirth, showing you photographs of your nude ass up against his roommate's ass; lifeless pink; panties on the floor; extinguished. A fluid in you circulates as quickly as the image through the listserv did. Your laugh makes a breached blue body. Fold limp. Is it colding? Is it end yet? You're trash mute; dumpster foul; rock hammer wasted.

[WITHIN A WEEK SHE WAS ROTTING FROM THE INSIDE]

++

Within a week, you start to smell a wanton smell. This smell is not your smell. It is as though wherever you go, an aura of sewage follows. You smoke, strain, float, cheef, change the channel, hit the blaster, pass whatever faster, faster, until your midriff reeks the undeniable: a tarnished molten marrow. A rancid roadkill arising. It is as though you hadn't already burrowed it into the carpet. You step into the shower, turn it hotter, shards of water running down your rabid dog leg. Lift it up; press your heel harder into wall. Press it breathless; press it endless pushing, push it; is; coming; coerce it; moan; moaning more; mourning the emergence of some meaning; seen; clean crown of proof. You give birth to the ugly cotton truth; tar covered gum song; the lost tampon; the last symbol; the collapse down on shower floor; sob. Sob; sob.

[AND THE HOLLOW FIGURE BROKE TO PIECES ON THE FLOOR]

++

Sometimes late at night, you can feel a terrific movement in your underbelly. A radiance swells & swells & swells & swells. You cannot hold you like this. How is anyone supposed to hold you like this. It keeps you, it keeps you like this: awake, away from sleep. You think, *if I could just*—you think—*just jab some holes*—you think—*so it can bleed*—you think—*& leave.* You get out the tweezers while your roommate dreams you dig & dig & dig & dig until you recognize a round grief. It is gowned in red & hiding an ingrown nothingness. You wash the tweezers, set them down on the counter, turn the bathroom light off. The nothing leaves. *Finally,* you say & fall asleep.

[DESTROYING ALL TRACE OF HER PASSAGE]

++

What is upside down of enough? Where the implication of fullness is neither empty, nor bursting, but an invisible plodding along. Keeping on. Never jolting enough to rip. Your image spins & trips into kaleidoscopic montage. Your eyes in the mirror beg for stability. Beg for constancy. We have a hard time locating you. So you neutralize your nails & lips, powder away your nose, conceal any freckle, every redness. All other imperfections, all aberrations must go. Bit by bit we decompose your image. Lay wire to a complex compulsion of cover, compulsion to be anything but in refusal. To be what you might be would be too much. To un-see what you are seeing you crease your eyelines in coal, blink side to side until a subtle greyness bleeds into your periphery. The rest of your face sits back, blank to stare. Fade out.

[THIS WAS THE ORIGIN OF HER FORTUNE]

++

Sh

the

She

the

Sham of me.

[SHE ASKED TO KEEP IT UNTIL THE RAINS WERE OVER]

++

You are inside a bile cocoon. You do not know your gifts from your wounds. Your fingers from your own netted ankles. There is only one face in the world that you can count on & it is not yours so do not glance into the mirror as the lights go out. When the lights go out you fall into a familiar dark florescence. You fill up your solo cup again. Magenta stained tongue slip. Sip. Sip. The juice begins to leak down your leg & you let it. Stay; you are already so adapted to obscurity. You stay despite the black light; despite the already standing four walls you erect & you erect & you erect more walls between us; I cannot possibly see in but still you warn me not to look. Sip. I look away. Bodies slip in & out through the door; you are a silhouette among other crawling, creeping silhouettes. You are nothing; an invisible radiation. You tilt your head back; you try to relax into the question; you think of the clear object; you think of all the vile places you've never been to. You long to make yourself a place. You long to go now.

[AND THE BIRDS WILL COME TO FEED]

++

Shame of the shame.
Shame of the
shame. Shame of
the shame. Shame
of the shame.
Shame of the shame. Shame
of the shame. Shame of
the shame. Shame of the
shame. Shame of the shame.
Shame of the shame. Shame.
of the shame. Shame of
the shame. Shame of the shame.
Shame of the shame.

[SHE SECRETLY TOOK MARROW SYRUP & PUT HONEY ON HER EYES]

++

You are dressed in high black boots. I was told I had to be tender. I so want to be tender with you. Like time how it attends to its matter like a gardener; knowing in the midst of weeding that what plagues us guides our growing; rinse. I wince; it makes a wind at which you squint. You look up; discreetly see; and we are equally surprised; rise. It's been so long since I have seen into your eyes; they are even & brief; a moment of pause; in passing we aid & form; a metallic drop between us; some sustenance; the size of a stone fruit & amber. It is just enough nutrients, you decide, to get you through the rest of this feverish night.

[OVERCOME BY AN EXPLORATORY DELIRIUM]

++

You feel dirty when you open your eyes to stare at the ceiling. There isn't far to look. There isn't much light yet. Your phone is on the floor, hopefully. Across the room your friend tosses a pillow over her head. You close your eyes into last night's whirlpool of streaked faces & cheap liquor & no oneness. All morning you try to dream about the right future, but something vague blocks any imaging. You are too bloated to try harder, you fall back asleep.

[WITHOUT LOSING THE POISE OF A WILD BEAST IN REPOSE]

++

You need to go home. You dread going home. You crave the warmth of brick, potato bread, that purple door. The way moisture ladles itself into your bones. Whether hot weather, whether cold; this is your own humidity; a dire humility; your vulnerability pains me
as you enter through the garage, take off your scarf, set down your bags. You haven't eaten a thing all day woke up hungover took speed drank three large coffees smoked weed hit the road for four-hours-forty-five minutes zoomed home.
So quick! Your mother greets you with an embrace as solid and profound as her natural stature will allow. *You look great,* she says earnestly. *Are you hungry?* Her compliments scratch a strange itch; feed a subtle gust of pride inside your chest. This is your own fragility.
These are your own tall trees reaching skyward without leaves; this is your own brutality; whose edges against the plush mouth of atmosphere make you lay on your yellow carpet & stare; stare. For endless hours their height holds above you, balanced on the very verge of crumble;
you find your self strung up among those frozen branches; hanging far above & looking down; down; towards the tiny quivering specimen of your body, laying far beneath you in your bed; waiting for sleep.

[AS IF ONLY WAITING FOR IT TO CLEAR]

++

Do you want something to eat? Your mother asks again and again. You feel it lurch, but do not feel hunger. Maybe you relabeled the sensation, so any wanting translates gnawing into growing. Any emptiness translates to good girl. You get yourself a plastic cup & fill it with water, lean. Your waist against the island, break. Into pieces, dip. Sigh.

[AND ALL THE CLOCKS STRIKING AN INTERMINABLE HOUR]

++

Sometimes you find yourself hiding inside a morsel of your own toe, staring out & up at the grandiosity of your whole physique. You especially delight in these moments, where it feels probable to exist inside an atom of flesh, a matter so perfectly miniscule, no one would ever mind you. You like to linger here until your extremities tingle; lack of oxygen; lack of fresh blood; lack of you; lacquered through; almost dyed you try to linger but something swims you back; into the whole being there laying; drifting into dream.

[A NOCTURNAL BUTTERFLY FLUTTERED ABOUT HER HEAD]

++

Once in a burnt orange haze; there you were, churning the subtle scent, the kind that escapes from beneath the door when you are touching yourself. It sort of settles there; lingering; breathless like a signpost. Too silent. Are you coming? Are you calling? Are you pushing me away? Say it. Say my name, say a name, any name, gently, gentle, you are never kind enough; not with yourself, not with me, pushing so hard so hard, all our distances go numb, the whites of your eyes rolling forth, begging me to say your name. Still, nothing becoming fulfilled, nothing enough being explored, the pain turning into stasis instead of servicing any rupture. The burnt orange radiates, fumes circulate around the room in closed circuit. They're starting to get to your head. You go dizzy & it all builds up & stacks & presses against your rounded stone walls & there is never never never any rupture. Time is running swiftly out. You are never gentle; never enough; you don't deserve a name so no one knows it, so no one writes it, so no one speaks it, even badly. You are just kind of there sometimes, kind of elsewhere usually, splicing into various events, finding yourself dressed up for the occasion; syncing your body among; between. Right in the middle, hoping no one will look. You tell your body it belongs here, to this throng of other bodies, as your body glitches in & out, longing to believe you.

[WITHIN THE LABYRINTH OF HER MADNESS]

++

It's a sappy Southern end of August & you want to go to the quarry but you wish you
could go to the quarry all by yourself you wish you didn't wish this you wish you could
be easy but you can not you have to make it all so drastically
tragic so hard you bad you have to
be shy you have to be closed
clothed coded you
have to be
you have
to be you
have to
you can't
be you
can't be you.

[SHE FOUND THE STITCHES OF THE VEIL]

++

Sh.

Ha.

Am.

Me.

[A MARGIN OF LUCIDITY]

++

I should be here, you think. And the assertion rises like a fire snake through your torso. *I deserve to be written here,* you think, chiseling tiny divots into your desk. In anger, the snake grows an erection in its mouth, exposing its forked tongue, sticking out, quivering towards the tree. You see the low bottom of the fig, round, boisterously bending the branch with its gravity. You wish to bend like that. To have an ass that can like that. You could, you honestly *could* resist this urge; but you don't want to. You reach out. You reach & open your palm to find the letters of your name raining soft through outspread fingers and into a textbox of an open thread: discuss. *I should be here,* you think, *because I am here,* you declare, and we press enter.

[GREEDILY SHE ENGORGED WITHOUT RESTRAINT]

++

T

a k e.

[AT ONCE EVERYTHING UPSIDE DOWN]

++

You are on top of your mountain & you bite into a date. Your fingers look fleshy; foreign; as they grasp the shriveled casing. The sugar tastes your tongue before your tongue can brace itself, jaw widens as inbuilt knowledge pours & heart purrs. Throat swallows new altitude. You squeeze & swell along the torso in rhythm to a sweet humming; the vent; the refrigerator; the city outside as quiet witness & even she cannot see you through small well of fire escape window; so you are free to undulate your awe. The last of the fruit dissolves unto your tongue & dries your mouth. You water. You water you. Wetter, you crescendo. You pause & look around. You emerge back into material.

[THE WORLD WAS SO RECENT THAT MANY THINGS LACKED NAMES]

++

A

h.　　　　　S　　　　　*h.*

[SUCH WAS THE PRESTIGE OF THAT SILENCE]

++

You find a way to leap; a temporary leave; a stint abroad in Scandinavian cityscape. Here, there are so many ways to escape, but less the reason. Still, you find your way through to the main drag of freetown borough where everything is vegetarian, anti authoritarian & semi legal. You lay yourself back in the grass. The hash highlights tension in your spine, like one thousand little fruit flies percolating beneath the skin of your hips. You unpad your lips. Open & close your jaw, rolling from side to side on the short dry lawn of the mound like a dog trying to find its right shape. In your mind this is the perfect place to be swallowed; surrounded by tall green reeds & open open open enough to stretch out within; humming enough to daze into; and even almost dozing, if it wasn't for the spiked heads of the short blades, of the sepia sodden grasses, sticking into, the fabric of your pants, keeping you just awake. You bend the right knee & straighten out the left. Turn anew; elbow up; cheek into your other hand. *Ah.* The weight of everything flickers.

[AND ALMOST AS COOL AS WATER]

++

For once, it feels so comfortable to be you.
In this straw berry belly of a cloud.
You had suspected its lingering; voraciously prayed to pull to pull it
down from; out of & in to;
the open open flesh & bone & mudmess of the world.
Into your curves your curls your holes your eyes
in question of the world.

[SHE HAD BEEN ABLE TO LEAP OVER THE WALL]

++

You want desperately not to feel bad about this propensity for slipping; for it feels so much like nothing & why should nothing not be good? You think: *why should I want to feel anything?* At least you think you thought so, but instead of existing in your mind the thought occurs outside of you & you see it hanging there in front of your face, spinning around itself, like the diamond shaped curser in that computer game. Mesmerized by its orbit, you stare until you are only a pair of eyes & then no eyes & then no I for a moment it is just the reeds framing your singularity. But what's yours must belong to a you & every you knows a thing or two & the thing your you knows well is that you can never ever stay in your own absence. At least you've never been able to stay; what a shame; all too quick; you remember your density & you come to.

[SHE DID NOT KNOW EXACTLY WHEN SHE BEGAN TO FLOAT]

++

By November, it is dark for eighteen hours of the day. Through the darkness yellow rectangles glow. Yellow rectangles pepper the dark, you think, with a kind of omniscient glowing. You walk through the dark & count one; step step; two; step step; three four five. The rectangles figure at pleasing angles. You observe as you step, step across the cobblestone, winding your way through the streets. You look up towards the skyline & three rectangles glow back in recognition. It's not as if you are only starting to notice, but a little like the noticing has become mutual. Since you vowed yourself to this more profound looking, certain shapes have declared their allegiance. Certain colors, certain light. You have never been so certain of sight. You do not miss the sun, but there is a free solar bed in the gym & it remembers warmth to your skin as you listen to the same mandolin over & over & over; the sounds themselves make a home. Your home is not here, but it isn't back in any of the *theres* you've ever lived in. It is more likely somewhere within these strings, and if you listen enough times with enough concentration you might finally sink enough to stay.

[HER IMAGE FADED INTO A UNIVERSE OF UNREALITY]

++

The song ends & you cannot stay. *You can never stay,* you think as you continue down the cobblestone through darkness, in rhythm to the sounds of this clean clean city & the bleating of your bodily fluids. It is hardly night; but already the quiet people have taken underground, opened their bottles, set flame to their candle sticks, turned their ovens on low to roast. You marvel at their ability to slow. At the yellow light, yellow lean of their lamps lacing where their curtains cannot hold. I gently guide you; closer; you ripple; at my tender pressing, crane your neck ever so slight a recognition of my presence. Silent we; move through the city; look down by the soles of your shoes; there is one faint rectangle glowing at ground level. A subtle radiance exudes as your passing feet step, step fast. I beckon you to pause. You would love to pause. You would love to dip down & out of your darkness into someplace radically calmer; yellower. You would love to go under, find someplace new. Walk in through cellar door, already an old friend, fingering tiny pastries off waiting tea trays, talking until resonance leaks a melody. How we would sit together in ambience 'til morning breaks but step, you cannot stay. You cannot stop, step, step. You keep moving.

[SHE DID NOT LET HERSELF BE DEFEATED BY RESIGNATION]

++

You step onto the metro, it is sterile. You sit anywhere you like, it is brazen white, there is plenty of room. The few faces ignore your arrival, look down at the clean clean floor to avoid possibility of any interaction. You ride static, feet firm on the ground as the metro slides the rail with taunting ease. You can only wish to move along so easily. What right would you have to gazelle. What right do you have to sire. To ask for what the fibers of your flesh have been itching towards. O bold desire. Something is coming & *could it be yours?* Would you were to demand it. The metro stops. Your feet carry you onto the platform, down each of the sleek stairs, across the pebbled terrace, beyond the parallel road, out onto the concrete that quiet carries you home. You ascend the elevator, open your own door, fall to your knees & plead to me. Please. Please *send me.*

[SHE BEGGED ME FOR A NAME]

++

She of

of my.
Ah. Sh.

She of
of my.

Ha. Shem.

[WHEN IT WAS ALL OVER, SHE LOOKED THE SAME AS BEFORE]

++

You return for graduation; it is finally hitting; it is over. As is tradition, celebration floods the shore all through the week. Asphalt prods your bare toes as you make your way over; soles tickling with a low-grade burn. Like most things, you are unsure if it hurts until you're off of it and safely onto the next texture. It is ten a.m. & scattered granulars of sand press excitedly into the bottoms of your feet. All around your circumference, your ends redden & twitch. This sun-dripped coursing of adrenaline tells you *it* is finally *hitting; it is beginning.* Designer drug disperses through your bloodstream; you feel it sifting through your capillaries; masquerading as tiny particles of oxygen; engaging the interest of your lungs. You walk along the blue slatted path in concentration; it narrows & elongates as you near the powdered mouth of the beach.

[NOW HER LUNGS WHISTLED AS SHE BREATHED]

++

Out across the body of the sea you see the lady parts of a mythic mammal. She is beating in the wind, or perhaps her pulse is the wind's own source. She is competent, rhythmic, powerful. You are drawn to her sensually. You match your pulse to her bleating blue pulse and look: she is natural she is metal she is voluptuous she is so blustery your underbody salivates & you smell your own feral smell & it smells synthetic like you want to be freer but not until tomorrow like you want to be bigger like this high up all the time crown nearly brushing me with artificial reach but you just can't stay you just can't shake this ragged tired shaping. Can't shed here. Not after all this stale time.

[SHE WAS MOVED BY HER OWN INNOCENCE]

++

It's so hot you become your own bead of sweat. Slow metallic glide, you slide yourself down the opal of a shoulder. Your shoulder. You should have told her how smooth her shoulder was to slip across. Leaving you translucent in lines of littered wetness, you trace your own silhouette down down chasing the next bead of sweat down your arm, which is you too. Both beads & both arms & every grain of sea glass sharded beneath you, the towel between your cells & the sand of you squeezing a handful until it all sifts outward; the cracks between your fingers become sieves. You look up.

[ONLY THEN DID SHE LEARN THAT HER VERSES HAD NOT BEEN BURNED]

++

Your friends' legs lengthen into laugh-o-dills,
their stems make slender shadows which seem to shelter you from the heat.
She throws a frisbee & it's course curves into a wide horseshoe,
you watch intently
as the tip of it comes close to your nose, you squint your eyes
willing it to stop;
it pauses midair:
what almost held it there?
We tilt back into play.

[SHE SAW A LIGHT RAIN OF TINY YELLOW FLOWERS FALLING]

++

The sky is tilling itself greener; you take your glasses off & look & put them back on & look again at the one cloud that looks like a dragon until the whole tail of the thing twirls out into a new dispersal of white vapor; you try to decipher its figure but it evolves with a new sense of speed, never resting in any one decision of a shape. Never holding still. You consider your own distribution, relax into old indecision, decide you are still learning how to circulate.

[A HEREDITARY MEMORY IS TRANSMITTED]

++

We are on top of our mountain & the flora goes sepia. The garden embraces our falling memories; dreams; prayer; regrets; a new current winds; a tunnel spreads; across; between; all identity relinquishing hold; a wormhole holds itself open. I escort you down the spiral stairs; *hello hello;* generations sing a prayer in tired unison; *yes, we have felt this before,* a bright lubrication of what is still alive inside. We hum as we help her off the concrete; as we clean the blue internal broth of leaken entrails off the floor, brush her hair; sponge her warm; ask her name. You and I unite inside the question; inside the hearing of each other's ancient asking. Here, I unveil the bread as if an answer; two candles reclaim your lace. Cue alora; cue catharsis; torrential disappearing of the hard stuff; our embryonic future spinning over in soft whirlwind. Cue letters of; cue scars from; drainage of pent up misery gone; tumble into new world slow; weaker hues of purple; cue rain; and rain. Whose ovals are framing our face? I see hands are these our hands, whose hands, whose fingers sweeping inwards of the flame; whose fingers pressing eyelids down to close; whose fingers cueing welcome, cueing home.

ACKNOWLEDGMENTS

++

I am indebted to Gabriel Garcia Marquez, whose *One Hundred Years of Solitude* accompanied me through the shadowed labyrinth of return & brightened this particular adventure of healing. All individual chapter titles are bibliomanced (with some revision) from his book, except "Greedily She Engorged Without Restraint," which is borrowed from John Milton's *Paradise Lost.*

"Within a Week She Was Rotting From the Inside" is a loose reworking of "Sewage" which appeared in *Black Candies: Gross & Unlikeable* (So Say We All, 2016).

The epigraph is borrowed from *Pyschomagic: The Transformative Power of Shamanic Pyschotherapy,* by Alejandro Jodorowksy.

"*Get up & fly away,*" are, in this case, lyrics from The Grateful Dead's "Wharf Rat."

I'd also like to mention the concept of *effortless perfection,* only directly referred to once, but underscoring the atmospheric pressure of the entire manuscript. This silent credo has been acknowledged, researched, and written about quite widely. For starters, see: *Women's Initiative Report,* Duke University (2003).

I am immensely grateful to poetess & confidant Marie Conlan, who pressured me into allowing this work to emerge, and sat and held these pages when I could not. To the Naropa JKS community, and .OFF conspirators, especially Danielle Ferrara, Jenni Ashby, Simone Liggans, Jes Davis, Shawnie Hamer, Jake Grieco, Karolina Zapal, Ryan Mihaly, Megan Heise, Sarah Richards-Graba, Serena Chopra, Jeffrey Pethybridge: thank you for the ecosystem of your friendship, radical thought, & constant poetry.

Thank you to the courageous teachers who model in real time a true possibility of healing; who have shown me how to live in my body, and how to be both tender & fierce with my own integration: Cheryl Deer, Jambo Truong, Ana Forrest.

Big gratitude to the ones who were there and still are: Ambrose Brooks Sheela, Julia Hawkins, Chelsea Ursaner, Reed Few, Allie Prater, Rachel Diamond, Christina Faidas. Thank you always to the beings who have harnessed and sustained me through all my many mutations: Mom & Dad. And of course and forever, to my Oliver. I love you, and our family of fur creatures.

And, special thanks to Ornithopter Press and Mark Harris for believing in & breathing life into this manuscript.

ABOUT THE AUTHOR

++

Gabrielle Lessans is an experimental poet whose writing orients toward the hearth where deep play & healing most intersect. She lives in Denver, Colorado with her husband, dog & two cats, leading weekly writing workshops, teaching yoga, and co-collaborating with Nocturne School of Lucid Writing and collective.off. She received her BA in Literature from Duke University and her MFA from Naropa's Jack Kerouac School of Disembodied Poetics, where she worked with the poetics of friendship, trauma and memory. Gabrielle was named a finalist for the Nightboat Poetry Prize in 2017 & 2018 for her collection *[a go]*. Recent work can be found in ***Black Sun Lit: Vestiges 4, Inverted Syntax, Dream Pop, Bone Bouquet.*** This is her first book.

www.ingramcontent.com/pod-product-compliance
Lightning Source LLC
LaVergne TN
LVHW080921110826
845155LV00039B/123
9781942723103